1 & 2 Thessalonians, 2 & 3 John, Jude

The Coming of
The Lord

S0-DOO-234

Neighborhood Bible Study Publishers
Dobbs Ferry, New York

The Coming of The Lord

ighborhood bible studies

11 Discussions for Group Bible Study
Marilyn Kunz and Catherine Schell

Copyright © 2001 by Marilyn Kunz and Catherine Schell

ISBN 1-880266-38-5 (Previous edition ISBN 0-8423-0424-X)
First Printing 2001
Printed in the United States of America
Cover by Tom Greene

CONTENTS

This study guide uses the inductive approach to Bible study. *It will help you discover for yourself what the Bible says.* It will not give you prepackaged answers. *People remember most what they discover for themselves and what they express in their own words.* The study guide provides three kinds of questions:

1. What does the passage say? What are the facts?

2. What is the meaning of these facts?

3. How does this passage apply to your life?

Observe the facts carefully before you interpret the meaning of your observations. Then apply the truths you have discovered to life today. Resist the temptation to skip the fact questions since we are not as observant as we think. Find the facts quickly so you can spend more time on their meaning and application.

The purpose of Bible study is not just to know more Bible truths, but to apply them. Allow these truths to make a difference in how you think and act, in your attitudes and relationships, in the quality and direction of your life.

Each discussion requires about one hour. Decide on the amount of time to add for socializing and prayer.

Share the leadership. If a different person is the moderator or question-asker each week, interest grows and members feel the group belongs to everyone. The Bible is the authority in the group, not the question-asker.

When a group grows to more than ten, the quiet people become quieter. Plan to grow and multiply. You can meet as two groups in the same house or begin another group so that more people can participate and benefit.

Tools For An Effective Bible Study

1. A study guide for each person in the group.

2. A modern translation of the Bible such as:
   New International Version (NIV)
   Contemporary English Version (CEV)
   Jerusalem Bible (JB)
   New American Standard Bible (NASB)
   Revised English Bible (REB)
   New Revised Standard Version (NRSV)

3. An English dictionary.

4. A map of the Lands of the Bible in a Bible or in the study guide.

5. Your conviction that the Bible is worth studying.

Guidelines For Effective Study

1. Stick to the passage under discussion.

2. Avoid tangents. If the subject is not addressed in the passage, put it on hold until after the study.

3. Let the Bible speak for itself. Do not quote other authorities or rewrite it to say what you want it to say.

4. Apply the passage personally and honestly.

5. Listen to one another to sharpen your insights.

6. Prepare by reading the Bible passage and thinking through the questions during the week.

7. Begin and end on time.

Helps For The Question-Asker

1. Prepare by reading the passage several times, using different translations if possible. Ask for God's help in understanding it. Consider how the questions might be answered. Observe which questions can be answered quickly and which may require more time.

2. Begin on time.

3. Lead the group in opening prayer or ask someone ahead of time to do so. Don't take anyone by surprise.

4. Ask for a different volunteer to read each Bible section. Read the question. Wait for an answer. Rephrase the question if necessary. Skip questions already answered by the discussion. Resist the temptation to answer the question yourself.

5. Encourage everyone to participate. Ask the group, "What do the rest of you think?" "What else could be added?"

6. Receive all answers warmly. If needed, ask, "In which verse did you find that?" "How does that fit with verse...?"

7. If a tangent arises, ask, "Do we find the answer to that here?" Or suggest, "Let's write that down and look for the information as we go along."

8. Discourage members who are too talkative by saying, "When I read the next question, let's hear from someone who hasn't spoken yet today."

9. Use the summary questions to bring the study to a conclusion on time.

10. Close the study with prayer.

11. Decide on one person to be the host and another person to be the question-asker for the next discussion.

T his letter testifies to the power of the gospel of Jesus Christ to transform lives. The missionary team of Paul, Silas and Timothy spent only about three weeks in Thessalonica in the early summer of AD 50. As they explained the Scriptures about the Christ (the Messiah), some Jews and many prominent Gentiles believed in Jesus. Jealousy prompted other Jews to instigate a riot, forcing the missionaries to leave the city. In the next six months, however, news of the converts' faith and transformed lives spread all over Macedonia and Achaia (present day northern and southern Greece).

Concerned for these young Christians after the missionary team had to leave them so quickly, Paul sent Timothy back for news. Timothy returns to report their strong faith in spite of continuing persecution. He also brings Paul the questions that trouble them. About six months after he left them, Paul writes from Corinth to encourage the Thessalonian Christians and to answer their questions. Many think this is the first letter we have of those Paul wrote to the young churches he founded in his journeys.

As You Wait For the Son, Be a Model

1 Thessalonians 1

Parents are often shocked when a child mimics their words and tone of voice exactly, or a boy walks and gestures just like his dad. These parents have been models of more than they knew. Families, society and the church are looking for positive models.

1. Think about someone who has been a model for you. What qualities of that person do you try to imitate? Why?

   The church at Thessalonica is only about six months old, but Paul commends them for their positive example to other churches. Look for ways these Christians are a model for you and for the church today.

Background: Read Acts 17:1-10

2. Where, when, and what, does Paul preach in Thessalonica (verses 1-3)?
   In Jewish synagogue

---

3. Who responds positively to the news about Jesus (verses 2-4, 9b-10)?

many Jews. Greeks. prominent women

What negative responses do some make, and why (verses 5-9)?

Jews were jealous & formed a mob to start a riot - seized Jason

*Note: Verse 4, **God-fearing** (NIV), **devout** (NRSV), people who followed the Jewish religion to some extent without being full converts.*

4. What positive and negative responses to Jesus do people make today?

5. If you were one of the new believers in Thessalonica, what emotions would you feel during the riot and as you help Paul, Silas and Timothy to escape (verses 5-10)?

Read 1 Thessalonians 1:1-10

6. After Paul had to flee Thessalonica, the young church receives this letter. From the tone of the letter, how would you describe the relationship between Paul and these new believers?

very affectionate & warm
strong affection - brothers

7. What do Paul, Silas and Timothy remember about the Thessalonian Christians as they pray for them?

remembers accomplishment of faith
hard work of love

T. turned to Christ in faith - served him out of love - born persecution patiently.

faith love & hope — 12 — essence of God.
given life in Christ.

How does becoming aware of a person's spiritual life and values affect your relationship?

8. What examples have you seen of *work produced by faith, labor prompted by love,* and *endurance inspired by hope*?

9. Why is Paul so confident that the faith of these Christians is genuine, not just an emotional high (verses 4-6)?

God chose them a gospel came to them in power & Holy Spirit paul didn't convince them by words- Holy Spirit brought them to chirst.

10. How would you describe the Holy Spirit's role in your spiritual journey?

11. Why may suffering and joy come together when someone welcomes the message of Jesus (verse 6; Acts17:4-10)?

Welcomed the gospel even w/ threat of tribulation- joy of their forgiven sins.

12. In what ways are the new believers imitators of Paul and of the Lord (verses 5-8)?

joyful in the gospel, persecuted for belief Paul taught with his life as well as his words.

13. What two things have become known because of these Christians in Thessalonica (verses 7, 8)?

were a missionary church.

their faith has spread the Word of the Lord Examples to other new christians as well as to non-believers.

What part have hearing the message and seeing a person of faith played in your responding to Jesus?

14. What joyous experience do these missionaries describe in verses 8b, 9?

Became a model for all. Word has resonated. so effective that Paul's evangelism no longer necessary.

15. From verses 9, 10, find at least six things included in the Christian message.

welcomed Paul w/ love   turned in faith to christ   Jesus who rose from dead
serve the living & true God   Jesus forgave our sins
wait for Jesus return

How would you describe the past, the present, the future of these Christians?

The fury of a loving God to all that distorts & defaces his world Hope of J's imminent return.

Summary

1. What impresses you about these Thessalonian Christians?

2. Which of their qualities would you like to see in yourself and in your church?

Prayer

O God, thank you for the example of these young Christians in their joy and faith, their love and endurance as they declared your message in what they said and how they lived. Make me aware that I am a model to someone of something. What I look like, what I say, what I do, what I value, what I believe—I am an example for good or for ill.

Help me to value what you value. Strengthen me to serve you, the living and true God, as I wait for your Son from heaven. Amen.

As You Wait For the Son, Seek the Praise of God, Not Man

1 Thessalonians 2:1-16

W ho doesn't like applause, or acclaim? The supervisor's commendation is a welcome sound. A job well done at home, school, church, or work deserves praise, but a good deed may go unnoticed or be misunderstood. Then we have to ask, who am I trying to please. God knows the deed and the motive behind it. Is pleasing God what really matters?

1. Think of a situation when you had to choose between pleasing God and pleasing people. How did you decide what to do? Or, what do you wish you had done?

Paul's goal was to please God who tests our hearts. He was persecuted, falsely accused and misunderstood, but never enslaved to earning human praise. Paul's example demonstrates the perspective and the confidence we need to live a life that wins God's praise.

Read 1 Thessalonians 2:1-12

Even though he suffered at Philippi, he continue to preach boldly & exuberantly

2. In verse 2, Paul refers to suffering at Philippi. Locate Philippi in Macedonia on the map on page 67. Read Acts 16:11-40 to discover what Paul and Silas had suffered, and why.

   At what point would you have been tempted to quit?

3. If verses 3-6 are an answer to accusations against Paul, Silas and Timothy, what has the opposition been saying?

   Paul was trying to deceive or trick people or convince people to worship wrong God.

4. To answer such charges, how does Paul describe his motives and actions (verses 4-6)?

   His message was true, his motives pure & methods straightforward. He behaved as a faithful servant of God - to please God, not men

   How would knowing that you are *approved by God to be entrusted with the gospel* and you are trying *to please God*, affect your witness for Jesus?

5. From verses 7-9, what picture do you get of a wise Christian witness and leader?

   gentle. loving. devoted & loving - willing to share gospel & their lives.

6. What difference does it make in your attitudes and behavior if you know that the person speaking or writing to you genuinely cares for you and desires the best for you?

7. How is Paul's concern not to be a burden, further proof of his love for these people (verses 6b, 9)?

Didn't look for recognition - worked + labored hard day - night not to be a burden

Note: Paul was a tentmaker by trade, work that could be done anywhere in Macedonia and Achaia. (Acts 18:1-4)

Worked w/ hands to earn what he needs Hard physical labor.

8. Paul keeps involving his readers: **you know, you remember, you are witnesses** (verses 1, 9, 10, 11). What had they known and witnessed about Paul's character, attitudes and ways of helping them?

He cared deeply for them - tender, self-sacrificial love (mother), kindly like a father - guiding them by his example

9. As their spiritual father, how had Paul dealt with these young Christians when he was at Thessalonica (verses 11, 12)?

Encouraged them strengthened them taught them about ways to behave in a manner worthy of God,

In what ways has another Christian done any of these things for you?

not rules ordained by Caeser or false idols' requirements but reflecting God's glory

Read 1 Thessalonians 2:13-16

10. What characterizes the ways that the Thessalonians had responded to Paul and his message (verses 13, 14)?

They accepted it - sensing it was a divine revelation rather than human philosopy. God's Holy Spirit used the message to transform them.

11. What example have you seen of people responding like this to the message of Jesus?

12. How is the suffering of the Thessalonian church like the suffering of the churches in Judea (verses 14-16)?

*The ssalonians being persecuted
~ suffered for their faith.
Judeans rejected message of Jesus ~ continue
to reject claims of early Jewish xtians*

Note: Locate Judea and Jerusalem on the map on page 67. Jerusalem is the city where Jesus was killed and the church began.

13. How can we be sure that we are helping, not hindering, another person's spiritual growth?

14. Summarize the good news and bad news in this paragraph.

Summary

1. List the characteristics of a wise Christian witness from Paul's example.

2. Which are most important to you? Why?

Prayer

God our Father, I am challenged by Paul's eagerness to please you even when others falsely accused and misunderstood him. I am touched by his blameless behavior toward the young believers at Thessalonica. Like a mother, he gently cared for the church, and like a wise father, he encouraged his children. He wanted your praise, not the praise of anyone else.

I confess, Lord, that the praise of people is often more important to me than your praise. Your church in every generation suffers persecution, humiliation, and opposition. You have entrusted the gospel to us. But how much inconvenience and embarrassment am I willing to face to communicate the gospel to my generation? Forgive me, Lord Jesus. Help me to be like Paul and these early Christians in their faithful service to you. Amen.

As You Wait For the Son, Anticipate Great Joy.

1Thessalonians 2:17—3:13

On New Year's Eve, crowds line the sidewalks in Pasadena, California to get a prime viewing spot for the Rose Bowl parade the next morning. They carry sleeping bags, food, beverages, chairs, cots, and whatever they need for the long night. In a festive atmosphere, they anticipate the joy of a close-up look at the breathtaking beauty of the lavish flower-covered floats.

1. What events have you anticipated with great joy?

Paul, greatly concerned that he could not return to Thessalonica, has sent Timothy to them in his place. The ways Paul describes the Thessalonians' importance to him give new meaning to the word *joy*. Consider what you learn about a person by knowing what gives him joy.

Read 1Thessalonians 2:17-20

2. Why does Paul have a mixture of frustration and joy? *He was with them for a short time - snatched away. Longs eagerly for them*

satan got in his way

3. If someone wrote these things to you, what would you know about your value to that person?

4. How does the picture of what will happen when Jesus comes, surprise or encourage you?
Paul's eagerness for Jesus' coming includes his pride in their development - faith - his crowning glory.

Read 1 Thessalonians 3:1-5

5. Why did Paul send Timothy back to visit Thessalonica? *He couldn't bear it any longer - he sent Timothy to bring his letter of encouragement + comfort & also to obtain news of the church*

6. What impresses you about the description of Timothy and his task (verses 2, 3)? *strengthen them   keep them focused   bring comfort   on set path   encourage them so persecution would not discourage*

7. When he was with them, how had Paul tried to prepare the young church to face trials? *them   Reminded them persecution normal experience for christian*

8. What could be the possible effects of trials and persecution on new Christians, then and now? *Paul is afraid of them abandoning their firm hold on gospel - can't bear thought that his work in Thesal. might be for naught*

9. When you are facing trials or ridicule for your *naught* faith, what would a visit from a "Timothy" mean to you?

How can you be "Timothy" to a member of your group or your church as they face trials or ridicule?

Read 1 Thessalonians 3:6-10

10. How does Timothy's news of the steadfastness of these young Christians, affect Paul (verses 6-10)?

He is encouraged
He now is able to continue (to live) if they stand firm in their faith.

11. You learn a great deal about a person's value system by observing what makes him happy or sad. What do you learn about Paul and his companions from what causes their joy or sadness?

12. What would someone learn about you by noting what makes you happy?

13. When Timothy assures Paul of the Thessalonians' love for him, what are Paul's new prayer requests (verse 10)?

He prays earnestly for them night & day to be reunited & to encourage their faith

Note: After only a few weeks in Thessalonica, Paul and Silas were forced to flee for their lives because of opposition from some of the Jews. The bond Jason and his fellow Christians had to post with the city officials apparently prevented Paul and Silas' return.

Read 1 Thessalonians 3:11-13

15. Put Paul's three prayer requests in your own words.

How do these requests reflect your basic needs as a Christian?

16. What perspective on your ultimate goal and hope does verse 13 give you?

Note: **Holy ones** *may refer to angelic hosts attending Jesus' return, or to believers who have already died.*

Summary

1. Trace the expression *your faith* in 1 Thessalonians 3:2, 5, 7 and 10. How can the members of your Bible study and/or your church express similar concern for each other?

2. The early Christians joyfully anticipated the Lord Jesus' return. From these first three studies, what do you learn about that event and how to live in expectation (see especially 1:10; 2:19; 3:13)?

Prayer

Lord Jesus, please make my love increase and overflow for others. I want to devote my thoughts and emotions, my values and energies to the things that you value. Strengthen me to live to please you, that I may be blameless and holy when I face you at your coming. Teach me to live in anticipation of that joy and glory. Amen.

As You Wait For the Son, Live to Please God

1 Thessalonians 4

We want to please the people we love. We also want to please ourselves, and sometimes, the crowd. Pleasing God often conflicts with these desires. Every day provides choices as to whom we will please.

1. How do the ways that Christians handle sexual temptations, love each other, and do their jobs, demonstrate their eagerness to please God?

As in Thessalonica, living in a sex-saturated culture makes immorality an acceptable lifestyle. Believing that Jesus may return at any moment, prompts some Christians to quit work. Other Christians worry about what happens to believers who die before Jesus returns. Each of these issues offers choices for pleasing or displeasing God. Each issue also influences the respect unbelievers give to the young church.

Read 1 Thessalonians 4:1-8

2. From verses 1 and 2, what was the aim and authority of the instructions Paul gave the new Christians?

   urges them in Jesus Christ - authority
   to please God - aim

   Even when we are doing right, why do we need urging to do so *more and more*?

   focus inspiration encouragement

3. A frequently asked question is, "How can I know the will of God for my life?"

   From verses 3-8 list what is God's will for every Christian?
   sanctification, abstention,
   self-control, to be holy + honorable,
   love one another, to be accepting +
   present w/ God

   Note: Be Sanctified means to be set apart, to belong to God, to be holy, to show the same character as God.

4. How is a Christian's sexual behavior to differ from that of the surrounding culture (verses 4, 5)?

   to not be lustful like unbelievers

   What helps you learn to control your own body in a way that is holy and honorable?

5. How do verses 6-8 emphasize the seriousness of these instructions?

   the Lord is an avenger

6. What connection do you see between the Spirit whom God gives to Christians and the kind of life God calls you to live (verses 3-8)?

Read 1 Thessalonians 4:9-12

7. After complimenting the Thessalonians on their love of their fellow Christians, what three commands does Paul give them (verses 11, 12)?

   to live simply, to mind own affairs, to work with hands, to be independent & behave rightly

8. How could their expectation of Christ's imminent return cause some young Christians to act in ways that would lose the respect of society, or cause financial problems?

9. Loving Christians want to help others in need. How can following the instructions of verses 11, 12, keep us from creating dependency in the people we want to help?

Read 1 Thessalonians 4:13-18

10. What apparently has Timothy reported to Paul about what is troubling the Thessalonian Christians?

    They are worried about those who've died before second coming.

11. What assurance does Paul give them about believers who have already died (verses 13, 14)?

    Jesus will raise up those who have died.

12. Notice that Paul does not say that Christians are immune to grief. But how and why do Christians grieve differently from other people?

    Because we have hope

13. List the sequence of events described in verses 16 and 17. *The Lord with a cry, a call + a trumpet will descend from heaven, + the dead in Christ will rise first. Then we will be raised to meet them in heaven.*

*Note: **To meet the Lord**, verse 17: In the Greek speaking world of that day, when a king paid an official visit to a city, leading citizens and chief officials went out to meet him. They escorted him on the final part of his journey into the city.*

What does this add to your understanding of Paul's comments on Jesus' return?

14. How can you use verse 17 to encourage one another when you grieve?

    We will be reunited in eternity

Note: For more information about the Lord Jesus' return and the resurrection of believers in Christ, read 1 Corinthians 15, and 2 Corinthians 5:1-10. Paul writes more on the subject in 2 Thessalonians.

Summary

1. Paul's instructions about *how to live in order to please God* include sexual morality, love for fellow Christians, and work. How can your behavior in these areas win respect or disrespect from unbelievers?

2. How do verses 13-18 help you face fears about your own death, or about the death of a loved one?

Prayer

Dear Lord, I really like those Christians at Thessalonica. They seem so eager to please you. Help me to be more like them in my desire to be holy, to understand your will and to do it. Thank you, Lord Jesus, that we can live in expectation of your return, when all believers will rise to meet you and be with you forever. Amen.

As You Wait For the Son, Have No Fear of Death

1 Thessalonians 5

In "Out of Africa", Isak Dinesen reports a conversation with her African servant after a death in the village. "Africans talk about death but fear to touch a dead body, white men don't talk about death but will touch a body."

1. Cultures and individuals handle the fear of death in different ways. What are some ways you see people cope with the fear of death?

The Thessalonians wondered about the date of Jesus' return. Would some of those living miss the coming of the Lord? Would believers who already had died miss the events of Jesus' return?

As Paul calms their fears and answers their questions, his words encourage us to live in joyful hope as we wait for Jesus to come again.

Read 1 Thessalonians 5:1-11

2. What do the two illustrations in verses 2, 3 indicate about Jesus' return? *the day of the Lord - thief in the night/labor pains*

   How do they emphasize the impossibility of escaping the events of the day of the Lord? *inevitable like the tides or night & day*

Note: The day of the Lord (verse 2) is an Old Testament term referring to God's future intervention in history both in salvation and judgment. In the New Testament, it designates all the events involved in the second coming of Christ.

3. On whom will destruction come, and on whom will it not come (verses 1-4)? *Those who are not believers. Children of the light will escape it.*

4. List the characteristics of the two different groups of people in verses 3-8. *children of light /day keep awake + sober* *destruction / no escape children of night sleep / drunk*

5. How are Christians to live until Jesus returns (verses 6-11)? *be watchful + sober faith, love & hope. armour.*

Note: The word sleep is used in three different ways in verses 6, 7, 10.

6. How can *faith*, *love* and *hope* defend you (verse 8)?

7. According to verses 9, 10, what benefits does Christ's death bring to all believers? *we may live with him.*

*Note: God's **wrath** (verse 9) is his permanent and consistent attitude, as a holy and just God, toward sin and evil. Until the final day of wrath, God's wrath is tempered with mercy, especially in dealing with his chosen people. Jesus experienced in our place the afflictions, punishment, and death that belong to sinners subject to God's wrath.*

Read 1 Thessalonians 5:12-22

8. Paul gets very specific about how to please God and to encourage one another. How would his commands help members of a church fellowship:

    In relating to their leaders (verses 12, 13)

    In relating to each other (verses 13-15)

    In their worship (verses 19-22)

9. What clues do you observe in verses 12-22 about the temptations these young Christians faced?

    Which do you meet today?

10. Paul and Silas have earned the right to have their commands in verse 16-18 taken seriously. (Review Acts 16: 22-25 if needed.) How do these commands compare to your idea of the will of God for you?

What is the difference in being joyful, praying, and giving thanks *in* all circumstances rather than for all circumstances?

Read 1 Thessalonians 5:23-28

11. What do you learn about God, and what he will do for those he calls (verses 23, 24, and 4:7)?

What do you want to say to God in response?

12. How does this prayer summarize what every Christian needs?

13. What do verses 25-28 tell you about the relationship Paul and his companions have with this young church?

Summary of 1 Thessalonians

How does your anticipation of Jesus' return affect the way you live?

1 Thessalonians 1:9-10 *turn to God & serve him*

2:19 *paul's hope & joy is the faithful Thessalo*

3:12, 13 *The Lord increases our love for one another & will keep us blameless*

4:13, 16-18 *the Lord will descend. raise the dead & all those alive*

5:2, 9-11 *the day will certainly come the Lord died so we may live w/ him We encourage & love one another w/ that goal*

Prayer

Lord Jesus Christ, though we don't know the time you will come again in power, we thank you that your return is certain. Keep us from thinking and living as if this world is all there is. Help us to balance our present responsibilities, with watching for your return.

God of holiness and peace, make us joyful, thankful, prayerful people. Keep each of us blameless in our whole being—spirit, soul and body, at Jesus' coming. We are so glad that you are able, and faithful to do this. Amen.

More news from Thessalonica has reached Paul in Corinth. The young Christians are speculating about the sudden return of the Lord. Some have become idle since they expect that Jesus may appear at any moment. Others are troubled by persecution. Paul writes this letter shortly after his first to clear up their misconceptions.

Paul encourages these young Christians to focus on their immediate responsibilities as well as on the future glory of Jesus' return—a wise balance for Christians in every generation.

As You Wait For the Son, Trust God's Justice

2 Thessalonians 1

Christians today in Nepal, India, Indonesia, Sudan and other countries face persecution for their faith. Some are denied education and jobs because they are Christians. Families may reject them and issue death threats. Their homes and businesses are destroyed. Some face police questioning, torture and prison. Yet God loves them, sees the injustice and asks them to trust him.

1. How do you resist the temptation to pay back trouble to people who trouble you?

Trouble and injustice force these early Christians to choose how they will react—in anger and revenge, or with growing trust in God's loving care. Paul encourages them trust God who is just.

Read 2 Thessalonians 1:1-4

2. What do you learn about the senders and the recipients of this letter (verses 1-2)?

Note: **Grace** *was the normal greeting with which letters between Greeks always began.* **Peace** *was the normal greeting between Jews.*

3. Read verses 3 and 4 in several translations. How would you feel if you received this message?

4. While the young Christians are being persecuted, what is happening to their faith and love?

How do you account for this?

5. What are the missionaries telling other churches about the Thessalonian Christians (verse 3, 4)?

Give examples of Christians today enduring persecutions and trials for their faith.

Read 2 Thessalonians 1:5-12

6. What do the Thessalonians' perseverance and faith prove about them?

What does it mean to be *worthy* (verses 5b, 11)?

7. Paul declares that *God is just*. What do you learn about his justice from verses 5-10?

8. Who will suffer punishment and why (verses 6, 8)?

   What does it mean to *not obey the gospel of our Lord Jesus?*

   How is obeying the gospel related to knowing God? (1 Thessalonians 1:5, 9, 10)

9. In verses 7 and 10, Paul gives new information about the day *when the Lord* Jesus *is revealed from heaven*. What will that day be like for those who have believed the gospel of the Lord Jesus?

   For those who have not believed?

10. In light of God's judgment Paul prays for these young Christians (verses 11, 12). How do his requests fit their needs?

    Consider what *good purpose of yours* or *act prompted by your faith* you want to ask God to fulfill by his power.

11. How is the name of Jesus honored in of the lives of Christians you know?

Summary

How can this letter's perspective on God's justice help you when life is "just not fair"?

Prayer

Lord Jesus, my faith needs to grow, to be exercised and developed. My love for other Christians must increase. I need your power to face injustice. As I wait for your return from heaven, fulfill by your power every good purpose I have and every act that comes from faith in you. May your name be honored because of the way I live by your power and grace. Amen.

As You Wait For the Son, Don't Panic

2 Thessalonians 2

People predict the date of Jesus' return. The date comes and goes, leaving disillusioned followers who sometimes commit suicide. Doomsday stories, nuclear threats, and horror movies spread frightening ideas of the end of the world. Speculation abounds.

1. As you read or hear ideas about the end of the world, what questions or fears do you have?

False rumors about Jesus' return have alarmed and confused the young church at Thessalonica. In his letter Paul corrects false ideas and gives new information about what must happen before Jesus' return. Things will get worse but they don't need to panic. Jesus, who called them to share his glory, is in control.

Read 2 Thessalonians 2:1-12

2. What misunderstandings of Paul's teachings have upset these young Christians (verses 1-3)?

*Note: **The day of the Lord** includes many events. The report that these events have begun to take place (verse 2) would lead people to expect that the coming of the Lord himself and the gathering of believers to him would certainly occur shortly.*

3. Whatever report they have heard, what does Paul make very clear in verses 3, 4?

4. List everything you can about **the *man of lawlessness*** or ***the lawless one*** including things that will accompany him (verses 3, 4, 7-10a)?

Note: Verses 5, 6 refer to verbal teaching Paul gave while in Thessalonica to which we have no access.

5. Why is ***the lawless one*** not ultimately to be feared (verse 8)?

What impresses you about the means the Lord Jesus will use to destroy the lawless one?

Read aloud verses 9-12 in at least two translations

6. The *lawless one* will display *counterfeit miracles, signs and wonders* (verse 9). Why should Christians not be swayed or deceived by *signs and wonders*? (Compare Jesus' warning in Mark 13:21, 22).

   Give contemporary examples of people being swayed by false messiahs.

7. In verses 10b-12, notice the words *because, for this reason* and *so that*. Put in your own words the sequence of choices and the consequences they trigger.

   What human choice precedes God's actions here?

8. What characterizes those who *refused to love the truth* and *have not believed the truth*?

   Put in your own words the truth that must be believed.

   Acts 17:1-4

   1 Thessalonians 1:9, 10

   2:13

   5:9, 10

Read 2 Thessalonians 2:13-17

9. How has the mood in this paragraph changed from the previous section?

10. Why does Paul feel obligated to thank God for these Christians?

11. From verse 13, how would you describe God's part and our part in salvation?

12. What perspective and encouragement do verses 13, 14 give to Christians who are enduring persecution and suffering?

   Consequently, what actions are they to take (verse 15)?

13. How does Paul's description of God in verse 16 affect your confidence in God's power to *encourage your hearts,* and *strengthen you in every good deed and word?*

   Why do you need God's encouragement in both your heart and your actions?

Summary

How does this passage address your questions or fears concerning:

the future?

difficulties and suffering that may come?

Prayer

God our Father, help me to trust you for the future things I don't understand. Help me to concentrate on the things from this study that I do understand. Help me to stand firm in my faith in the gospel, and not be shaken by spiritual enemies and lies. Thank you, Lord Jesus, that you will destroy Satan and all his forces when you are revealed from heaven at your coming. Amen.

As You Wait For the Son, Don't Be Idle

2 Thessalonians 3

Paul set the rule, "If a man will not work, he shall not eat," because a lifestyle of idleness affects the church and its witness in society.

1. Why is idleness dangerous both to the lazy person and the congregation to which he or she belongs?

In Thessalonica some of the young Christians quit work because they expected Jesus to return at any moment. Perhaps they thought he would return before their bills came due. Maybe they thought the wealthier Christians would take care of them. Possibly they thought that it was more important to proclaim the Gospel to their neighbors than to earn a living. How should the church treat idleness or laziness? Ignore it? Treat the idle as the enemy? Provide for them when they won't work? Paul denounces idleness and the problems it creates. He sets an example by his own work and gives guidelines for a constructive solution to the problem.

Read 2 Thessalonians 3:1-5

2. The previous chapter closed with a prayer for the Thessalonians. What two things does Paul now ask them to pray for him and his companions?

   What insight do these requests give you into Paul's circumstances and his goals?

3. What balance do verses 3, 4 suggest between what God does and what a Christian does?

   Remembering *the lawless one* described in chapter 2, what can the promise of God's protection from *the evil one* mean to you?

4. How do you respond when someone speaks to you in the way Paul does to the Thessalonians in verse 4?

   Why?

5. What sort of evidence in the lives of these young Christians will show that God has answered Paul's prayers in verse 5?

Read 2 Thessalonians 3:6-15

6. In his previous letter Paul instructed the church to **warn those who are idle** (1 Thessalonians 5:14). Now what stronger actions does Paul order them to take (verses 6)?

    On what authority does Paul command them?

7. When they were in Thessalonica, why did the missionaries set the example of work that they did?

8. Why is the principle "If a man does not work, he shall not eat," important to the life of the church?

9. Contrast the two lifestyles in verses 11-13.

    What effect would each have on the church and its witness in society?

10. In verses 14, 15, how does Paul reinforce and clarify the command to **keep away from every brother who is idle** (verse 6)?

    What are the goal and the hope of these commands?

Read 2 Thessalonians 3:16-18

11. What does Paul emphasize in his closing prayer for this persecuted church, confused about the details of Jesus' return?

In what circumstances and times do you want to pray this prayer for yourself or for others in your group?

Note: Verse 17—This concluding note in Paul's own handwriting will guarantee its genuineness to those receiving it.

Summary

1. Look for ideas and encouragement for your prayer life from Paul's prayers in this letter:

   2 Thessalonians 1:3

   1:11

   2:16, 17

   3:1-5

   3:16, 18

2. Why does the church still need Paul's example and instructions about work?

Prayer

Father, there is a lot of "burn out" today, even among Christians. In evil times the temptation is to become weary in doing what is right. Lead us into a greater understanding and personal experience of your love and the endurance you give. Give us your peace at all times. Add to the numbers of those who serve you faithfully. Empower us to serve you and to communicate your message to our generation as we wait for your Son from heaven. In Jesus' name, we pray. Amen.

T he Apostle John wrote these brief letters toward the end of the first century. At that time traveling preachers visited widely scattered churches to instruct and encourage the new believers. The few inns were dirty and unsafe, and Christians provided hospitality in their homes for these teachers. But false teachers also traveled to spread their ideas about Jesus. In his letters John commends Christians for their unselfish hospitality to teachers of the truth, but warns against taking in false teachers. They need to show concern for both truth and love.

As You Wait For the Son, Balance Truth and Love

2 John and 3 John

Think of the way you handle conflict. Some personality types prefer to confront the issue, while others prefer peace at any price. Is the issue to clarify and correct error? Is it a matter of loving the person with whom you differ?

1. How do you balance truth and love? On which side of the balance scale do you usually find yourself— truth, or love?

In these letters John gives guidelines for setting a balance between love and truth. His warnings about false teaching and instructions about hospitality are strikingly contemporary.

Read 2 John

2. How does John identify himself and the recipients of the letter?

*Note: **The chosen lady** and her children may refer to an individual and her family or to a local church and all believers.*

3. John connects *truth* and *love* in verses 1-3. What does it mean to love someone *in the truth* (verse 1) and *because of the truth* (verse 2)?

4. In verses 4-6 what point is John making by his circular reasoning about love and commandments?

5. How does John's opening emphasis on *the truth* prepare *his* readers for the warning in verse 7?

6. What tests can Christians use to determine if a teaching is true? (Compare verses 3, 7, with 1 John 2:22, 23; and 1 John 4:1-3.)

Note: Some in the early church attempted to bring Gnostic teaching into Christianity. The Gnostics believed that the spirit is good, but the body is evil. Therefore, Jesus could not have been both God and man.

7. What false ideas about Jesus do you find in what you read, what you see on TV/movies, or in conversations?

8. How do the warnings and promises in verses 8, 9, motivate you to live in truth and love?

Note: John instructs Christians to deny hospitality to teachers who deny the truth about Jesus. But this does not include friends and neighbors who do not believe the truth about Jesus.

Read 3 John

9. Why does the news he hears about Gaius give John such great joy (verses 1-4)?

   Why does truth continue to be the writer's major concern?

10. What else do you learn about Gaius and the other believers from verses 5-8?

11. In addition to offering hospitality, what opportunities do you have to *work together for the truth* with church leaders and missionaries?

12. In contrast to the good example of Gaius, John describes Diotrephes. List five or six things you learn about him from verses 9, 10.

    What sort of things would Diotrephes do in a local church today?

13. What do the actions of Gaius, Demetrius and Diotrephes reveal about each of them?

14. Why is *peace* an appropriate benediction for Gaius, who faces the situation addressed in this letter?

Summary

1. What warnings do these two brief letters give against deceivers?

2. How can you blend truth and love in your conversations and relationships with those who do not believe the truth about Jesus?

3. These letters give examples of Christians who follow the truth and walk in love. In what practical ways can you follow their examples:

> in balancing truth and love in the family and the church?

> in offering loving hospitality, a place of welcome?

Prayer

God our Father, help me to walk in truth and love. Strengthen me to stand against those who try to deceive me and deceive others. Help me make the truth about Jesus clear in the way I live and what I say.

O God, like Diotrephes I am tempted to want to be first. Help me to put you and others ahead of myself. Forgive my hesitation to practice hospitality. You know my self-centered excuses. I want to love and obey you in sharing my time, myself, my possessions. In the name of your Son Jesus Christ, who is the way, the truth, and the life. Amen.

J ude's letter, written about fifteen years after Paul's letters to the Thessalonians, is not addressed to a particular church or individual. Jude writes to Jewish Christians of his day and to all Christians everywhere.

Traditionally, Jude has been recognized as the brother of James and half-brother of Jesus. James and Jude are named among Jesus' brothers (Matthew 13:55; Mark 6:3). Jesus' brothers did not believe in him during his lifetime, but at least these two believed after his resurrection (John 7:5; Acts 1:14). James became the leader of the church in Jerusalem and presided over the Council described in Acts 15 (1 Corinthians 15:3-7; Acts 21:18; Galatians 1:19; 2:9, 12).

As You Wait For the Son, Contend For the Truth

Jude 1-16

Deceivers and infiltrators in the church are not new. Paul, John and Jude all warned the churches about them. In our generation, news media report about proud religious leaders who fleece their followers and sometimes end their empire in a mass suicide. Biblical words and terms are redefined and expanded to support godless teaching and behavior. Jude instructs Christians to take a critical look at these leaders' life and words.

1. Why do you think people get tricked into following false ideas about Christian faith and life style?

Read Jude 1-7

2. What does the way Jude introduces himself to his readers indicate about him?

3. Read verses 1, 2 in several translations. By what three phrases does Jude describe the people to whom he is writing?

   How do these phrases compare to your description of yourself as a Christian?

4. Jude's letter differs from what he had planned to write because he now sees a clear danger to the church (verse 3, 4). What does he urge his readers to do?

5. Godless men have *secretly slipped* into the church. How would their actions and teachings distort and undermine *the faith once for all entrusted to the saints*?

6. In what ways is *the grace of God* sometimes changed *into a license for immorality* today?

   How are the uniqueness of Jesus Christ, his incarnation and deity, denied today?

7. In verses 5-7 Jude reminds his readers of three Old Testament events. In each case what is the sin, and the result of the sin?

How does each event relate to unbelief or immorality, the two errors of the false teachers Jude writes about?

Note: In your study preparation, you may wish to read these Old Testament passages:

Escape from Egypt and destruction—*Exodus 12:29-42, 51; Numbers 13:1,2, 25-33; 14:1-38*

Sodom and Gomorrah—*Genesis 18:20, 21; 19: 1-29*

Read 8-16

8. In spite of knowing about these Old Testament events, what three things are the infiltrators doing (verses 8, 10)?

9. Jude compares these troublemakers to three Old Testament individuals. What effects would attitudes like theirs have on the fellowship of the church?

Note: In your study preparation, you may wish to read the Old Testament passages about:

Cain, *who killed his brother in jealousy (Genesis 4:1-16)*

Balaam, *noted for his greed and for leading Israel into Baal worship (Numbers 22:1—25:9; 31:7-16; Revelation 2:14).*

Korah, *who led the rebellion against Moses, God's chosen leader for Israel (Numbers 16).*

10. Read verses 12, 13, in several translations. What six vivid metaphors does Jude use to describe these dangerous people?

What do you learn about them from each picture?

Note: **Love feasts** *in the early church were meals accompanied or followed by celebration of the Lord's supper (Eucharist).*

11. What ungodly speech and motives characterize these teachers in verses 14-16?

Why are grumbling and boasting equally damaging to a group of Christians?

Note: The book of Enoch is not included in the Jewish list of accepted Scriptures, but Jude assumes it is familiar to his readers and respected by them.

Summary

1. What examples of error about Jesus and about morality do you encounter in the church today?

2. Jude draws a graphic picture of deceivers who change the message of Jesus and advocate ungodly behavior. How can you protect yourself and other believers from these errors?

Prayer

Lord Jesus Christ, we don't often think about the need to guard against evil from within the church. But we recognize the things Jude mentions: unbelief, immorality, jealousy, greed, pride and power. Give us courage to resist these temptations and to stand against them in the church. For your sake and glory, Amen.

As You Wait For the Son, Build Yourselves Up

Jude 17-25 and Review

Remember how bits of advice pop into your mind at just the right moment? "Look both ways before you cross the street." "Jump feet first into water if you don't know the depth." "Unplug the toaster before you put in the fork to pull out the bread." "Turn off the engine before you pump gas."

Jude wants his readers to remember the advice that can protect them from spiritual dangers. To be forewarned is to be forearmed physically and spiritually.

1. How has someone's warning helped you to face temptations, doubts, or opposition to your faith?

After his graphic descriptions of the dangerous teachers who have slipped into the church, Jude affirms his *dear friends* who are contending for the faith. He tells them how to care for one another, the strong and the weak. He assures them of God's power to provide all they need and to present them blameless when Jesus returns. How appropriate Jude's instructions and assurances are for us today.

Read 17-25

2. What motivates and characterizes the scoffers the apostles predicted would come (verse17- 19)?

    How would remembering these things help the Thessalonian church then, and you now, when facing those who scoff at the Christian faith?

3. In contrast to the scoffers who don't have the spirit and follow natural instincts, what four things are Christians to do (verses 20, 21)?

4. What role does each person of the Trinity (*God, Son, Holy Spirit*) have in helping you to *build yourself up* in your Christian faith?

5. Read verses 22, 23 in several translations. In addition to nourishing their own spiritual lives, what responsibility in actions and attitudes do Christians have toward doubters and those following false teachings?

6. How can your attitudes and action help someone who is beginning to be deceived?

7. List all the things you learn about God from Jude's closing benediction (verses 24, 25).

   Do you think the **great joy** is our joy or God's? Why?

8. From this benediction, what new thoughts do you have about God, and about yourself?

Summary

How do the opening salutation and the ending of Jude's letter encourage you as you serve God and wait for Jesus' return?

Review of 1 and 2 Thessalonians, 2 and 3 John, and Jude

Paul, Silas, Timothy, John, Jude—all lived life in the light of the expected return of the Lord Jesus in power. Christians today can keep their balance in unsettling times and difficult situations because of their confidence that the Lord Jesus ultimately will bring everything under his glorious power and authority. Meanwhile we love and serve Jesus Christ as we await his return.

1. This guide is subtitled *The Coming of the Lord*. Like each major Christian doctrine, the second coming of Jesus has at times been neglected, and at times overemphasized. In every generation Chris-

tians need reminders that the world as we know it will end. The time is coming when God will intervene in power. Then every knee will bow and every tongue confess that Jesus Christ is Lord.

Review the following verses, commenting on the impact of each reference as you go along:

1 Thessalonians 1:9, 10

2:19, 20

3:11-13

4:16-18

5:1-4

2 Thessalonians 1:5-12

2:8

3:3

2 John 7

3 John 3, 4

Jude 21, 24, 25

2. What practical difference will your knowledge about the return of the Lord Jesus make this year in your priorities, your anxieties, your behavior?

Prayer

To him who is able to keep us from falling and to present us before his glorious presence without fault and with great joy—to the only God our Savior be glory, majesty, power and authority, through Jesus Christ our Lord, before all ages, now and forevermore! Amen.

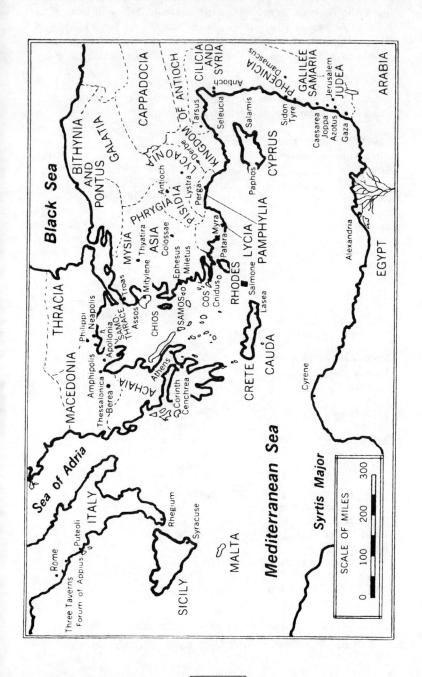

We recommend the Gospel of Mark, the fast paced narrative of Jesus' life, as the first book for people new to Bible study. Follow this with the Book of Acts to see what happens to the people introduced in Mark. Then in Genesis discover the beginnings of the world and find the answers to the big questions of where we came from and why we are here.

Our repertoire of guides allows great flexibility. For groups starting with *Lenten Studies*, *They Met Jesus* is a good sequel.

Level 101: little or no previous Bible study experience

Mark *(recommended first unit of study)* or
  The Book of Mark *(Simplified English)*
Acts, Books 1 and 2
Genesis, Books 1 and 2
Psalms/Proverbs
Topical Studies
Conversations with Jesus
Lenten Studies
Foundations for Faith
Character Studies
They Met Jesus
Four Men of God
Lifestyles of Faith, Books 1 and 2

> **Sequence for groups reaching people from non-Christian cultures**
> Foundations for Faith
> Genesis, Books 1 and 2
> Mark
> The Book of Mark
> *(Simplified English)*

Level 201: some experience in Bible study

John, Books 1 and 2	*Topical Studies*
Romans	Prayer
Luke	Treasures
I John/James	Relationships
1 Corinthians	Servants of the Lord
2 Corinthians	Coping with Stress
Philippians	Work – God's Gift
Colossians	Celebrate

Level 301: more experienced in Bible study

Matthew, Books 1 and 2	*Topical Studies*
Galatians & Philemon	Courage to Cope
1 and 2 Peter	Set Free
Hebrews	
1 and 2 Thessalonians, 2 & 3 John, Jude	
Isaiah	
Haggai, Zechariah, Malachi	
Ephesians	

Biweekly or Monthly Groups may use topical studies or character studies.

1-800-369-0307 • www.NeighborhoodBibleStudy.org

About Neighborhood Bible Studies

Neighborhood Bible Studies, Inc. is a leader in the field of small group Bible studies. Since 1960, NBS has pioneered the development of Bible study groups that encourage each member to participate in the leadership of the discussion.

The mission of Neighborhood Bible Studies is to:
Enable people to investigate the Scriptures
Encounter God in Jesus Christ
Mature in their faith

The vision of Neighborhood Bible Studies is to:
Change the World
One neighborhood at a time
Through the study of the Bible

Publication in more than 25 languages indicates the versatility of NBS cross culturally. NBS **methods and materials** are used around the world to:
Equip individuals for facilitating discovery Bible studies
Serve as a resource to the church

Skilled NBS personnel provide consultation by telephone or e-mail. In some areas, they conduct workshops and seminars to train individuals, clergy, and laity in how to establish small group Bible studies in neighborhoods, churches, workplaces and specialized facilities. **Call 800-369-0307 to inquire about consultation or training.**

About the Founders

Marilyn Kunz and Catherine Schell, authors of many of the NBS guides, founded Neighborhood Bible Studies and directed its work for thirty-one years. Currently other authors contribute to the series.

The cost of your study guide has been subsidized by faithful people who give generously to NBS. For more information, visit our web site: www.NeighborhoodBibleStudy.org.

COMPLETE LISTING of NBS STUDY GUIDES

Getting Started

How to Start a Neighborhood Bible Study *(handbook & video)*

Bible Book Studies

Genesis, Book One *Beginnings with God*
Genesis, Book Two *The Shaping of a People*
Psalms & Proverbs *Perspective and Wisdom for Today*
Isaiah *God's Help Is on the Way*
Haggai, Zechariah, and Malachi *Prophets of Hope*
Matthew, Book One *God's Promise Fulfilled*
Matthew, Book Two *God's Purpose Fulfilled*
Mark *Discovering Jesus*
Luke *Good News and Great Joy*
John, Book One *Believe and See*
John, Book Two *Believe and Live*
Acts, Book One *A New Beginning*
Acts, Book Two *Paul Sets the Pattern*
Romans *A Reasoned Faith...A Reasonable Faith*
1 Corinthians *Finding Answers to Life's Questions*
2 Corinthians *The Power of Weakness*
Galatians & Philemon *Fully Accepted by God*
Ephesians *Living in God's Family*
Philippians *A Message of Encouragement*
Colossians *Staying Focused on Truth*
1 & 2 Thessalonians, 2 & 3 John, Jude *The Coming of the Lord*
Hebrews *Unveiling Christ*
1 & 2 Peter *Letters to People in Trouble*
1 John & James *Faith that Knows and Shows*

Topical Studies

Celebrate *Reasons for Hurrahs*
Conversations with Jesus *Getting to Know Him*
Coping with Stress *Insights from Eight Bible Leaders*
Courage to Cope *Uncommon Resources*
Foundations for Faith *The Basics for Knowing God*
Lenten Studies *Life Defeats Death*
Prayer *Communicating with God*
Relationships *Connected to Others: God's Plan*
Servants of the Lord *Living by God's Agenda*
Set Free *Leaving Negative Emotions Behind*
Treasures *Discovering God's Riches*
Work - God's Gift *Life-Changing Choices*

Character Studies

Four Men of God *Unlikely Leaders*
Lifestyles of Faith, Book One *Choosing to Trust God*
Lifestyles of Faith, Book Two *Choosing to Obey God*
They Met Jesus *Life-Changing Encounters*

Simplified English

The Book of Mark *The Story of Jesus*